IMAGES
of America

LONDON

IMAGES
of America

LONDON

Carl Keith Greene

ARCADIA

First published 1996
Copyright © Carl Keith Greene, 1996

ISBN 0-7524-0529-2

Published by Arcadia Publishing,
an imprint of the Chalford Publishing Corporation
One Washington Center, Dover, New Hampshire 03820
Printed in Great Britain

Library of Congress Cataloging-in-Publication Data applied for

Contents

LONDON LIONS MINSTREL

Produced and Sponsored By London, Kentucky Lion's Club

Reda Theatre Feb. 9

Southland Theatre Feb. 10

Benefit: *Underprivileged Persons of Laurel County*
London Lions Club Eyesight Conservation Fund

Before the shows became politically incorrect, the London Lions Club put on an annual minstrel show to raise money for their causes. This program cover is probably from the 1950 performance, directed by Charles Higgs, which featured as End Men, Jess Doan, Rufus Bruner, Gene Cook, and Jim Bowles. The chorus included Jack Timberlake, Don Chesnut, Bill Griffin, Harvey Rush, Calvert Little, Bob Herron, and Mabel and Billie Bryan Bruner. Specialty numbers were done by Bennie Cook, Dobbie Magee, Sue Buchanan, and others. Music was done by Charles Young and his Rhythmairs, which included Buddy Westbrook, Bert Cox, Kenny Shackleford, Gene Barnett, John Black, and Hic Hill Billy Sizzlers.

Introduction

Since before Daniel Boone and Dr. Thomas Walker made their way through the Cumberland Gap into Kentucky, folks have been visiting London. According to legend and some archaeological findings, Native Americans visited the area while hunting long before white men came to the banks of the Laurel River.

Not long after Walker and Boone and their companions blazed their trails through what is now Laurel County, there came a long line of settlers along the Wilderness Road.

While many passed through, a few stayed. And from those who stayed, London was born. She came into the world on March 7, 1826, the product of the Kentucky Legislature's carving up of Pulaski, Rockcastle, Clay, Knox, and Whitley Counties. On December 12, 1825, the legislature ordered Laurel County to be established, and the act took effect on February 13 the following year.

Those who set up the county's government met beginning on March 6, and on the second day of the meeting they voted to accept the donation by John and Jarvis Jackson of a plot of land for the county seat. That plot of land was named London. No one noted why the name of the capital of the British Empire was selected, but the common speculation is that it was because most of those who had the power to choose had British roots.

As the years passed, London grew. Electricity came to town, then the telephone. The railroad arrived in the 1880s. Public water lines were laid and sewers were built. The automobile was invented and flourished, streets were paved. Gas stations were built. Churches were organized. The Women's Club opened a library. A golf course was built and rebuilt. Soon there was an airport. Industries began to locate their plants here. The main north-south and east-west routes across Kentucky cross here and form London's Main Street.

Boys went and came back, or didn't, from World War I, World War II, and the wars in Korea and Vietnam. Doctors began their practices here and opened hospitals. The state and federal court system was established here, and many lawyers began their practices in the area. Public schools and a college opened their doors. Bridge clubs met. Football, basketball, and baseball were played. For most of her 170 years London has been just like any other small town in America.

But for those of us who grew up in London, there is nothing like her. This book is not an exact history; it is more than that. It is a piece of nostalgia. When I first decided to write the book I told only a few people. One of those was my friend, Judge R.W. Dyche. Rob looked over some of the photographs I had chosen and said in a wistful voice, "If we could just walk there again." I think that's what I had in mind with this book, giving myself, and those who wish for it, a chance to walk there again.

I haven't tried to be particularly objective in this book. I've chosen images from my collection of places that are here no longer, photographs that show London's people at major events in their lives and the life of the town, and photographs of people who were and are important to the life of London. And I've chosen photographs of places that were important to me in the earlier part of my life and people who I particularly remember from my years growing up.

Most of all, I've chosen photographs that will help us to walk there and meet those people again. And to those who read this book who have never before walked there, it may give an opportunity to appreciate London in her youth and develop a new appreciation for London as she is now.

London is not just a place, she is a state of mind. For those of us who grew up here, it is a hard place to leave. It is a place that calls us back time and time again. For those who move here it becomes a place hard to leave. And for those who must go, I hope this book will go with them, and be a reminder of London for years to come.

Nearly all the photographs are from my collection. I have borrowed a few, and those have been identified as donations. The pictures date from about the turn of the century to about 1974. The photographs in my collection have been gleaned from photographic archives, from collections rescued from the trash bin, from family collections given me by friends so that the photographs will be preserved, and from collections of postcards for sale in antiques stores.

Some of the photographs may be cracked, or spotted, or faded. That, alas, is the problem with old photographs. They have often been stored improperly, abused, and/or poorly processed in the beginning, causing them to eventually fade. I've chosen the best copies available. Some printed especially for this book from old negatives still are not pristine quality because the negatives are damaged. Therefore I seek the reader's indulgence in advance.

This book is dedicated to those who appreciate the history of London, to those who remember what it was like to walk the streets in the 1950s and 1960s, and even in the 1920s, 1930s, and 1940s, and to those who would like to walk there again.

One

Looking at London's Past

The heart of London is shown here in 1891 or 1892. This photograph by W.F. Benge shows the north end of the Catching Building (at right), apparently while the building was under construction. Its construction spanned the years 1891 and 1892, and it was the first building in London to cover an entire block. It was located between Fourth and Fifth Streets on the east side of Main Street. The Catching Building's three-story hotel portion burned in 1910 and was rebuilt immediately with two stories. The building just north of the hotel is the Hackney Bros. building. Just beyond that is a building with a "restaurant" sign and beyond that is the office of *The Kentuckian*, a newspaper of the day. This photograph is reprinted courtesy of the University of Louisville Photographic Archives.

On January 17, 1922, The Oleika Shrine Temple held a ceremony in London's downtown. These two photographs, presumably made by London's P.L. Young, show the festivities surrounding those ceremonies. This driver is passing what is now the Roscoe E. Magee Company furniture store. On the far left is the Pica Building, then housing the Barnett Hardware Company, and The Surprise, which sold fine millinery. The vacant lot is where the Milby law firm's office stands now.

This photograph, probably made on the same day as the previous one, shows the same block. The entrance to the Poynter Building, which then probably housed a drugstore, can also be seen. Note the Western Union sign sticking out from the front of the building. The gabled building on the right-hand side of the photograph occupies the same spot that Magee's does now.

These shots of the Catching Building, possibly taken on the same day, were probably taken after World War II but before 1949, since the 1949 remodeling of Begley Drug on the corner in the upper photograph hadn't yet begun. The garage sign in the lower photograph apparently indicated the Dyche's garage, located then where the *Sentinel-Echo* office stands now. The garage was at one time a Willys and Overland dealer. The men on the right-hand side of the lower photograph are sitting on the rock retaining wall that surrounded the Courthouse Square.

LONDON, KENTUCKY, U. S. 25

13101

This postcard view of Main Street looking north appears to have been made in the early 1940s. At the extreme right in the white building is the Krystal Kitchen and Pearl's Sweet Shop. To the left the tower and clock of the Laurel County Courthouse can be seen above the Jackson Building.

This photograph, a view looking south, was made at about the same time as the one above. A corner of Hackney's can be seen at left. Begley Drug, with its corner entrance, is also shown, followed by the Hotel London. The Eversole Building, still comprising three stories, is beyond the Catching Building. At right can be seen the Western Union sign in the Poynter Building and a drug store sign. The "garage" sign refers to a garage west of Main Street on Fifth Street.

Some time after 1948 this street scene looking north appeared on a postcard. The Ford on the right appears to be of 1950 vintage. London Drug is on the left. This time the brothers Fish and John Dyche (both in white shirts) are seen entering the store. In the basement of the Poynter Building is the Basement Barber Shop (with its proprietor, Lee Carter), and Tom Craft Insurance. London Hardware is easily visible beyond the drug store and telegraph office. Next are the Pennington Brothers' grocery, Golde's clothing store, Kroger's grocery, Kidd Bros., and Carl Weaver's pool room. Showing at the Reda Theatre are *The Mating of Millie*, made in 1948, and *The Duke of Chicago*. The Hotel Laurel and its Cafe and another cafe can be seen just south of the Christian church. Beyond the church are the 4-Paw Hotel and a Standard Oil service station. The taxis in front of London Hardware bear the Brown Cab logo. The east side of the street shows little change from how it appeared in the previous photograph.

This postcard view depicts the Southland Theatre, which is showing *The Decision of Christopher Blake*, made in 1948, and *Shadow of a Woman*. Recognizable only by the "Eat" sign beneath the theatre marquee is the cafe called The Grill. South of the theatre is the London Electric Company, the London Wallpaper and Paint Company, and located in the Odd Fellows Hall is the London Motor Car parts department. South of that is the London Motor Car showroom with the Ford sign above, and on the corner is the Hob Nob Cafe. The Odd Fellows Hall fell victim to a 1970s fire, and currently a pocket park called Odd Fellows Park fills the space. South of the Hob Nob is the Pica Building housing the Jones Store, a women's and children's clothing store, and the Western Tool and Automotive Company.

Street Scene - London, K... I-Y-2

By the time this photograph was made, the Southland Theatre had been destroyed in a fire. The picture must have been made sometime after 1952 because the Reda Theatre is showing Cornell Wilde in *Operation Secret*, a film made in that year. Beginning at the extreme right, we see the First Christian Church and across West Seventh Street the London Florist shop in the Hotel Laurel building. Adjoining the flower shop is the Greyhound Bus Station. The Hotel Laurel lobby is beyond that, as is United Auto Parts, a company started by Mark Watkins, the owner of London Motor Car. On the east side of Main Street Gilmore Phelps' London Electric can just be seen on the extreme left. It had moved north from its 1948 location. In 1951 the Southland Theatre burned. Next door to London Electric are Abe Nakdimen's Fair Store and the Corner Cafe. Barely visible in the Southland Theatre building is Barton's Jewel Box on this side of the unoccupied theatre lobby. By 1955 that lobby would be occupied by Barton's 5 & 10. Before the theatre burned, Henson's clothing store and photography studio had moved into the building formerly occupied by London Electric. After the fire, the Boston Bargain Store moved into the London Wallpaper and Paint location.

The Southland Theatre was one of southeast Kentucky's movie palaces. Seating several hundred people, it attracted visitors from the entire area. At 7 pm on Friday, April 6, 1951, while *Born Yesterday* starring Judy Holiday was showing, it caught fire. Luckily, none of the hundreds of people in the theatre were injured as they were evacuated. These views of the theatre on the morning after the fire were made by London's Raymond Asher, who kindly allowed us to make copies of them and include them here.

The above photograph shows the damage to the theatre lobby. To the left of the lobby is a portion of Barton's Jewel Box and a cafe called The Grill. To the right of the lobby is one of the shops adjoining the theatre. The photograph below shows a close-up of the interior of the lobby and the firewall that kept the fire from spreading into the Odd Fellows Hall and engulfing the entire block.

The London Wallpaper and Paint store was also damaged by the fire. Currently, the First Lady Beauty Salon occupies the space. Tommie Lynn's Design, a home fashion shop, is in the space between it and the theatre lobby which, on the night of the fire, was occupied by Henson's clothing store. Lena's Wedding Shop now occupies the theatre lobby area and Style Jewelers has replaced the jewelry shop and cafe north of the theatre lobby. Seven apartments were also damaged in the fire.

This view of the burned out Southland Theatre shows the enormity of the theatre and the extent of the destruction. Now Martin Cupp and Son furniture occupies the space fronting on Hill Street. There are also apartments and office spaces on the second floor of the Main Street portion of the building.

This photograph of downtown made in early 1961 shows the Catching Building just south of Begley Drug and the Hotel London. A portion of Brock's Variety Store can be seen on the extreme left. Emmitt Shearer Insurance is located in the store that had earlier accommodated Mullin's' Studio, Harvey Rush Jewelry, and Buck's Grocery and Meat Market. The Second National Bank occupies the next space and Daniel's Department Store, recently closed down, is on the corner of Main and East Fourth Streets. The First National Bank is across Fourth Street, with McHargue's dry goods store beyond it and Champion's Supply store located between it and the Krystal Kitchen. Located in the area, but not visible in this shot, was a Shell service station between the Krystal Kitchen and the federal building. Close examination of the right side of the photograph shows that the picture was made while the current county courthouse was under construction. The rock wall that surrounded the previous building is still in place, but the earth has been excavated inside it. Beyond the courthouse can be seen Westbrook's appliance store (which also sold bottled gas and provided a water softener rental service) and the "Reddy Kilowatt" sign of Kentucky Utilities. Now the entire block from East Fifth to East Fourth Street is occupied by the Cumberland Valley National Bank, the successor to Second National.

18

Two

Looking at
London from Above

Aerial and birds-eye views of towns make popular photographs, and we are fortunate to have access to a number of such views of London. This photograph, by W.F. Benge, included courtesy of the University of Louisville Photographic Archives, shows London in the 1890s. It was taken from a hill known at that time as Sandbank Hill, somewhere near the western end of what is now Thirteenth Street. Some of the major landmarks shown are as follows: the Ramsey/Randall Cemetery, at the eastern end of what is now First Street, is in the upper left-hand corner; below and to the left of the cemetery can be seen the rear and steeple of the First Christian Church; and the steeple of the Methodist church is to the right of First Christian's steeple, with the three-story Catching Building in the background.

This dim photograph, shot in 1907 somewhere around the Sue Bennett Memorial School (perhaps from the administration building), shows the Louisville & Nashville Railroad tracks as they cross Sublimity (West Fifth) Street at what is now Mill Street. Sublimity Street is the broad street that can be seen running from the lower left side of the photograph toward the top. At about where the street fades from view, the Methodist Episcopal Church, South, can be seen. The courthouse rises above downtown in the center of the background. An unpaved West Fourth Street can be seen to the right of the courthouse.

This 1925 photograph by P.L. Young, taken from about the same location as the photograph at the top of the page, shows that in eighteen years the landscape had changed considerably. By this time, the railroad tracks have disappeared. Situated on Sublimity Street is the Methodist Episcopal Church, North, with the inscription "MEC" that was left by an earlier owner. Further up the street a new M.E. Church, South, has been built. The "o" in the upper left shows the location of the new hospital that would be constructed by Dr. H.V. Pennington. To the right, the "x" under the "2" marks the new Baptist church, built in 1923, and the "PO" beneath the "3" indicates the location of the post office in the federal building.

House's Garage, opened by Matt House and later operated by his sons Fayette and Raymond, had a contract in the 1950s and 1960s to maintain the county school system's buses. The garage, with buses stored behind and in the lot below, can be seen at the intersection of First, Dixie, and Whitley Streets in the upper left. This early 1960s aerial view shows Dave Parman's City Grocery across the intersection from House's. The street extending from the bottom center of the photograph, diagonally to its intersection with Mill Street, is West Second Street. College Street can be seen running parallel to Mill Street in the upper right of the photograph.

Downtown was about to undergo major changes when this early 1970s aerial photograph was made. Today, three of the blocks on the east side of Main Street have totally changed. The Catching Building, opposite the courthouse, has been replaced by the Cumberland Valley National Bank building. South of it, the block with the First National Bank has been removed to make room for a new First National Bank building. Behind the federal building, on the tree-lined lot, the Pigg Home has been razed to create a parking lot. South of the federal building, the old home on a tree-lined lot has also been replaced with the National City Bank building. Across from that lot, the multi-gabled house on Main Street that was the site of Rawlings Funeral Home has been replaced with yet another parking lot.

Three
Walking Again
in Downtown London

The Wren Block, photographed here sometime after 1908, was replaced by the Hotel Laurel, which was demolished in the 1970s. The First Christian Church's new building is in the background. The streets are still dirt, but the sidewalk in front of the Wren Block seems to be paved. The window to the right of what seems to be a basement entrance bears the legend "T.G. Moren Coal Office," and a Singer sewing machine sign is hung next to the door. A sign advertising Singer sewing machines is also attached to the utility pole. A close look beneath the trees north of the church reveals the foundation of the 4-Paw Hotel.

The Parman family has provided clothing for Londoners for the past five decades. The photograph above shows the family clothing store in 1954. It was located in the middle of the block between West Fifth and West Sixth Streets. Robert Parman opened the business and soon his sons Jack and John joined him. Today, the business has expanded from a single space in the block to a large store comprising five spaces, and its name has been changed to Bob's Ready-to-Wear. The modern store, shown below in a 1970s photograph, is located in the shops that were occupied by Pennington Brothers, Golde's, Kroger's, Kidd Bros., and part of Carl Weaver's pool room that are shown in the photograph on p. 13.

Bananas were 9¢ a pound and ground beef 39¢ a pound when this photograph of the original Dyche Jones Food Store was made. Dyche Jones opened his first grocery store on December 12, 1934, when he was nineteen years old. Until a little more than a dozen years ago, when the last of his stores closed, he was active in the day-to-day operations of the stores, which grew at one time to a small chain of stores in several towns in southeast Kentucky. This store, pictured in the late 1950s, was on the corner of South Broad and Third Streets, behind the First Baptist Church. A second London store eventually moved into the building vacated by Kroger's on the corner of North Main and East Ninth Streets. Jones also ran stores in Corbin and Manchester.

Hoskins dime store was ready for Christmas when this early 1960s photograph was made. Owned by Mr. and Mrs. Denver Hoskins, the store sold toys, school supplies, housewares, and sundries. It stood on the corner of North Main and East Eighth Streets where Laurel Florist is now located. Mr. and Mrs. Clarence Patton owned and operated the store before the Hoskinses.

East Fourth Street became an extension of the Main Street shopping area. This 1959 photograph shows three of the businesses there. At the far left, Asher's Salvage Store was also one of London's record shops, owned by Mr. and Mrs. Ellie Asher. The Dollar Store, shown in the middle of the photograph, featured no items over a dollar. Tots & Teens featured frilly children's clothing as well as clothing for ladies.

The Laurel County High School band is shown here passing the Reda Theatre in the annual Christmas parade. The theatre was already closed when this early 1970s photograph was taken. Style Jewelers occupied one of the shops alongside the theatre, which was opened in the 1940s and demolished in the late 1980s. North of the Reda is the Parks-Belk Company, a department store with branches across the southeast. In about 1960 it was located in the building constructed by Mark Watkins for his United Auto Parts business and machine shop. Beyond that is the Hotel Laurel and the Christian church.

It was big news when the new one-piece Ericofon brand telephone hit London. This photograph from the mid-1960s shows Kentucky Telephone employees Willa Mae Irvin (left) and Pauline Black demonstrating the new phones at the phone company office.

Although today it only houses switching equipment and a small business office, for more than thirty years this building on North Main Street was the headquarters of the Northeastern Telephone Company, the Kentucky Telephone Company, and the Kentucky division of the Continental Telephone Company. This 1974 photograph, made after Continental had bought Kentucky Telephone, but before the name was changed, shows a sign touting the installation of a new switching and direct dialing system. London has had telephone service since 1887, when J.T. Williams installed telephones in his business and his home on Long Street in order to communicate between the two. By 1954 there were 1,913 telephones in Laurel County.

The Poynter Building was built to house a drugstore, and until the 1970s it featured drug stores, a cafeteria, and a dollar store. This early 1970s photograph documents its incarnation as London City Drug, a Rexall agency. By the time this picture was made the Basement Barber Shop had closed and Homer Hampton had opened a shop in the old Western Union office. Bertie Shomaker had moved her gift shop from the upstairs room alongside the Reda Theatre to the basement of the Poynter Building. Today, the law firm of Scoville, Cessna & Assoc. occupies the ground level and second story of the building. The basement is occupied by Commonwealth of Kentucky offices. The London Hardware building to its north had been converted to offices by the time this photograph was taken. It is currently unoccupied.

In the early 1970s, Food Fair, a Somerset-based grocery chain, occupied the building on the corner of North Broad and West Eighth Streets built by Rufus Moren in the early 1960s. After Food Fair moved out, the building housed the offices of the Laurel Grocery Company for a while. It was recently purchased by First Christian Church and converted to a fellowship hall.

Hackney's had been closed just a year or two when this early 1970s photograph was taken. The family-owned dry goods store had been in business since 1879 and in later years advertised itself as "Where Your Grandfather Traded." When it shut down it was probably the oldest family-owned business in town. The owners of the Roscoe E. Magee Company, a furniture and wholesale electrical supply company and another of London's old, family-owned businesses, bought the Hackney's building and expanded their business into it.

The Hamm, Milby & Ridings law firm now occupies the right-hand side of this building, that was occupied by R.H. Hobbs Co. in the early 1970s. Hobbs had expanded into the ground floor of the Pica Building by the time this photograph was taken. Apartments took up the second floor. The north side housed the Jones Store, a ladies' and children's clothing shop, for many years and the south side housed Basil Poynter's Western Tool and Automotive Supply. Poynter had moved his shop to a location in the block to the north by this time, and then back to both sides of the Pica Building in the 1980s. The Pica Building fell victim to a fire in the late 1980s and was rebuilt by its owners, Mr. and Mrs. Bobby King. It currently houses Carousel Florist, James Carnahan's law office, and Traveltime travel agency on the ground floor, and the Christian, Sturgeon and Assoc. accounting firm on the second floor.

The second Laurel County Courthouse is shown here probably in the 1930s. The courthouse was built in 1884–85 to replace the courthouse and jail built in 1826 by Jarvis Jackson. This building was erected by John W. Mullins for $16,350. In the late 1930s a stone bandstand was built. During the life of the London Firemen's Band (1932–38), the band played weekend concerts on the courthouse lawn. The courthouse stood on an elevated piece of land surrounded by a stone retaining wall. On the night of December 9, 1959, it was destroyed by fire.

It took a while to convince the voters of Laurel County to build a new courthouse, but by the time these photographs were made in 1961, construction was well under way. In the photograph on the left workmen have just nursed the lower portion of a concrete column into place. In the photograph on the right a loader operator demolishes the stone retaining wall that supported the land upon which the old courthouse was built.

This photograph shows the third of four column bases being lowered into place by a crane as the new Laurel County Courthouse is being constructed. The Colonial Georgian structure was designed by Bayless, Clotfelter and Johnson, Lexington architects. By the mid-1980s county and state government offices had outgrown the building and an annex was purchased on Broad Street behind the courthouse.

The United States Courthouse in London was built in 1912 and is reputed to have seen more moonshining trials than any other in the country. When this photograph was made, probably in the 1930s, the post office was located on the ground floor. A new post office was built in 1961. The district court was located in London as the result of the work of Congressman Vincent Boreing and his successor, Don C. Edwards.

When this photograph was made in about 1920, Thelma Black (left), Sallie Black (right), and the woman between them were unaware that they were standing near the place where the new post office would be built. To them it was simply the location of the E.A. Pollard home on South Main Street.

Forty years later the home was razed to make way for the new post office.

The new post office was dedicated in 1961. It served until 1991, when a new regional post office was built on KY 192, west of London.

Before operations were moved into the new post office, Postmaster Wilmer Boggs (right) and Thurman Herron (a letter carrier) checked out the new equipment.

In the photograph to the right, Assistant Postmaster Omer Wells (left) is selling stamps to R.C. Walker soon after the new post office opened. In the bottom photograph, Jack Phelps handles mail for a couple. Through the window at left can be seen the home that served as the Masonic Hall in the 1950s.

These Cub Scouts provided a color guard on the day the post office was dedicated. They are, from left to right, Kenny McCracken, unknown, Glenn Cornett, Dale McCracken, Roy "Scotty" McFadden, Terry Dixon, and Mark Adams of Pack 42 in London.

Jailer W.H. Barnett and Deputy Jailer Dan Miller pose in front of the Laurel County Jail. These men served from 1918 to 1921.

The second Laurel County Jail was on the corner of Broad and West Fourth Streets. It was built in 1874 and served into the 1970s, when it was finally replaced by a third jail, after much debate in fiscal court. The first jail was constructed on the Laurel County Courthouse grounds on Main Street.

Excavation for Laurel County's third jail had begun when the photograph above was made in the early 1970s. The new jail was near completion when the lower photograph was made. The third jail did not last nearly as long as the second, and it was replaced by a new facility in the early 1990s.

Four

Stopping by the Drugstore

Drugstores were the center of life in downtown London for years, with local business people stopping in for morning coffee and lunch. The Catching Building's ground floor had become the site of two drugstores, a bank, and the lobby of the Hotel London by the time this photograph was made in the early 1970s. Begley Drug had been on that corner since 1921, and Dyche Drug had been on the other corner since 1961. The Second National Bank had changed its name to the Cumberland Valley National Bank and Trust and had moved from one store room into two others in the building. The entire block was replaced by a new Cumberland Valley Bank building in the late 1970s.

The soda fountain at Begley Drug was the meeting place for many local business people in the mornings and for high school students after class. It is depicted in this photograph made just after the remodeling of the drugstore in June 1961. The soda fountain was an integral part of the drugstore from its inception and was managed by Carl G. Greene from 1949 until 1966. Following him as fountain manager was Frances Wilhoit.

This 1961 photograph depicts the prescription and cosmetic department at Begley's, featuring the latest in cosmetics and fragrances. Harry Houchens Sr. was the manager and chief pharmacist of the store at that time. Other clerks who worked in the prescription and cosmetic department included Hazel Banks, Janice Herndon, Irene Spurlock, and Daisy Greene.

The tobacco department at Begley's sold not only tobacco products but candy, photography supplies, radios, clocks, pens, and pencils. Throughout the 1950s and 1960s the department was operated by Jessie Chandler, Maude Brown, and Lottie Smith. The London store was the first one to open as part of a chain of more than twenty drugstores. The corporation sold out to the Rite Aid chain in the late 1980s.

This view of the back part of the store shows how the Begley chain was leading the way toward the conversion of drugstores from pharmacies with soda fountains to urban general stores with pharmacies. Note that the store featured lawn chairs, electrical supplies, light bulbs, and badminton sets, along with sickroom supplies, school supplies, and veterinary supplies.

The Dyche Drug Company, operated by Robert and Fish Dyche until the late 1980s, was the successor to London Drug. The Dyches began their career in the drugstore business at the London Drug Store in the Poynter Building. In the 1950s they changed its name to Dyche Drug, and in the spring of 1961 moved to this space in the Catching Building that had recently been vacated by Daniel's Department Store.

This Polaroid photograph, probably taken about 1957, shows Robert Dyche's children, Paige and Robbie, behind one of the counters at the drugstore in the Poynter Building. The man standing near the window that looks out onto Main Street is thought to be their uncle, John Dyche.

44

Mr. and Mrs. Robert Dyche stand in front of the prescription department on the grand opening day of the new Dyche Drug Store in the Catching Building with their children, Robbie and Paige. Robbie is now a judge on the Kentucky Court of Appeals and Paige is an educator in Danville. The necktie worn by Robert Dyche was to celebrate the grand opening.

At one of the service counters on the grand opening day at Dyche Drug the camera caught clerk Wilma Woodyard, Boots Dyche (with her back to the camera), daughter Paige, clerk Elizabeth Parman, and Robert Dyche (also with his back to the camera).

A little later, the photographer and Robert Dyche surprise Boots Dyche as she rings up money on the cash register. Also shown is Paige Dyche (with her back to the camera).

Five
Religion, Education, and Medicine

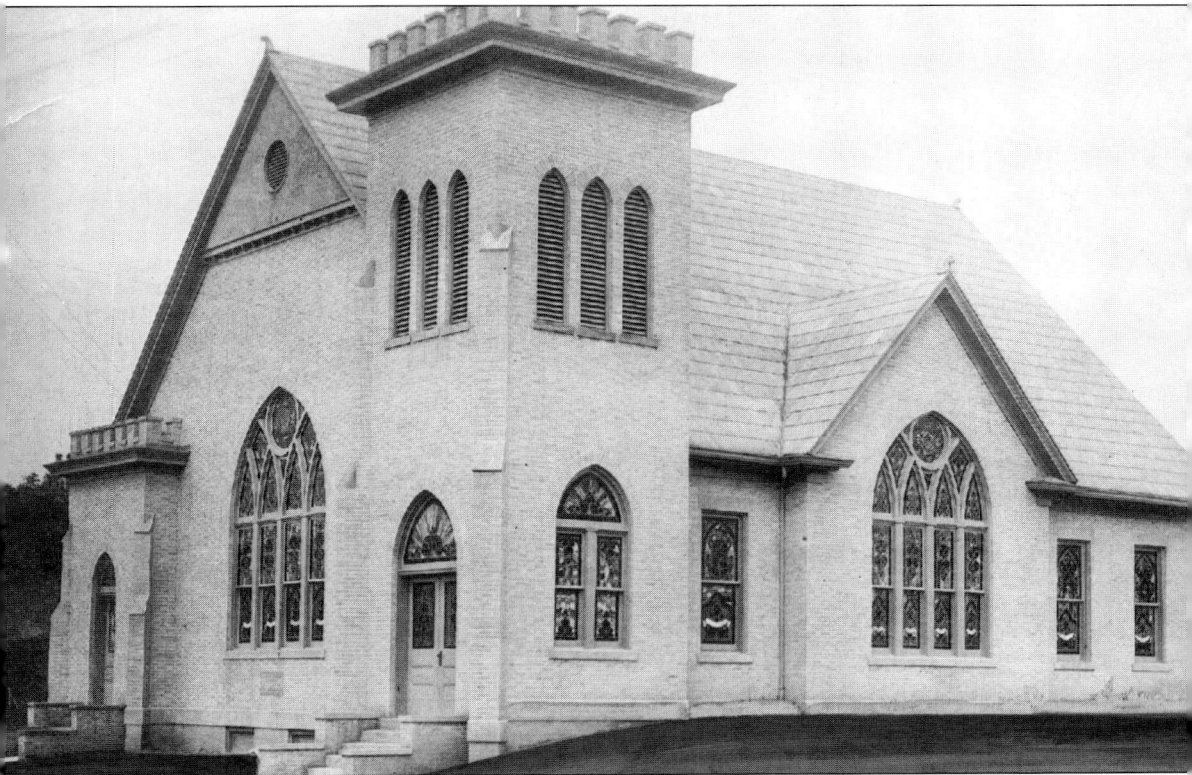

London has been a center for religion, education, and medicine since the early days. This is the Methodist Episcopal Church, North, in the 1920s. The church was built sometime after 1907 near the present-day intersection of West Fifth and North Mill Streets, and was used by the northern branch of the Methodist church until about 1939, when the northern and southern branches of the church reunited. The building was razed sometime after 1944, and the bricks were used to construct the home of P.P. Edwards, which is currently occupied by a law firm.

Possibly out on a Sunday afternoon outing, James M. Barnett (above left) was photographed with some friends at the Methodist Episcopal Church. His other friends in the photographs above, below, and on the next page are not identified.

The notes made on the back of this photograph do not include the name of this young lady, but they do include the date, January 1921, and the note "Just like I wanted it."

This photograph of the Methodist Church, South, appeared in a pamphlet published by *The London Sentinel* called *Views of London, KY., The City of Homes, Schools and Churches and Gateway to the Mountains*. The structure burned in December 1909, and was replaced with the church's current building in 1910.

The North Main Street Christian Church was established in 1888, and the current building was built in 1953. This photograph shows The Reverend Mr. and Mrs. Oldham, Christine Walker, and Charles Smith, sometime in the 1960s.

The African Methodist Episcopal Church was built on the corner of North Broad and West Eighth Streets in the 1920s. The congregation was established in 1884, but by 1954 it had not gathered for several years. The building was razed in the 1960s. This photograph also appeared in the *Views of London* pamphlet.

London's First Christian Church was built in 1908 and appears in the *Views of London* pamphlet. The congregation was organized in 1865 and built its first building on this site in 1870. That frame structure burned in 1907.

This view of the Christian church appeared on a postcard in the 1940s. Close examination will reveal that the upper portion of the front wall has been moved forward and two windows added on either side of the fan window. The wall was moved in 1943 to allow the installation of a balcony, the Sunday school office, and the pastor's study. Windows were also added to the towers to provide light and ventilation to the new offices.

The First Baptist Church moved into this building, shown in a photograph from *Views of London*, in 1894, and stayed there until it moved to the building on the corner of Main and Third Streets in 1923. In the early 1990s the church moved into a new building on West Fifth Street. The congregation was organized in 1885.

Pastor George W. Phillips, his wife Vada, and their sons Eldon and Leo posed in front of the rest of the congregation on April 2, 1950, after ground was broken for a new educational building to be added to the First Baptist Church's building, which had been constructed in 1923. The addition was completed and dedicated in 1952. Identifiable in the group are Cecil Yeary, O.H. Black, George Griffin, G.T. Lovelace, Jane Williams, W.T. and America Greene, Matthew Parker, Mr. and Mrs. Ernest Porter, Harry Snyder, and R.C. Miller.

Marymount Hospital as it appeared in 1949. The hospital was built in 1926 by Dr. H.V. Pennington and originally called Pennington General Hospital. In 1946 it was purchased by the Sisters of Charity of Nazareth. When it was built, it was the most modern hospital between Lexington and Knoxville, and was the only hospital housed in a building built specifically for that purpose in the area. Soon after this photograph was made the sisters added a convent to the top of the building, expanding it to four stories plus a basement.

Signing the contract to build a new Marymount Hospital in 1969 are, from left to right, as follows: (seated) architect Lon Fabian, contractor John Boggs, hospital administrator Sister Joseph Ellen Mara, and architect Joseph Potts; (standing) assistant administrator Ted Tieman and Woodrow McIntosh, chairman of the citizens' advisory committee.

Construction of the new hospital began with the building of concrete footers and the installation of steel reinforcements. This photograph shows the chaplain's home in the shadow of the hospital.

Soon after the foundation was completed, concrete was poured to form the floor of the basement and steel-reinforced columns were constructed to support the ground floor of the building.

This photograph shows the construction of the second floor about to begin, with steel reinforcement rods being laid prior to pouring the concrete for the floor. The building was completed in June 1971.

One of the features of the new Marymount Hospital was a modern laundry, which allowed the in-house cleaning of linen and other items. Shown with one of the new laundry machines are Ada Napier (left), Christine Humfleet (center), and Rachel Reed.

X-ray technician Betty Sturgill is shown supervising the installation of x-ray equipment in the new hospital. Marymount currently boasts the most modern laboratory and radiology departments in the area.

Sister Joseph Ellen Mara was the administrator at Marymount Hospital during the years of the construction of the new building. She was one of the five religious heads of the hospital after the Sisters of Charity of Nazareth bought it. She served as administrator for more than a dozen years, having come to Marymount in 1963. This photograph was taken at about the time she arrived there.

The old and new hospital buildings coexisted on the hill above London for several years. The old building housed the convent for the sisters, the headquarters for the county ambulance service, offices for Cooperative Church Ministries (now ComeUnity Cooperative Care), and other rooms that were sometimes used by the hospital. It was demolished in the early 1980s to make room for the first expansion of the new hospital. This photograph was taken in about 1974.

The first library in town was a small circulating library started by the ladies of the First Christian Church in 1915. It became a project of the Women's Progressive League and the Commercial Club, and in 1932, when the library received its own building, the London Women's Club took over its operation (the current library is built around that old library building). The photograph above shows the excavation for the second exterior remodeling. The first remodeling added a wing to the rear of the building; the second renovation added a second floor, and extended the front of the building to the street. The photograph below shows the new foundation and basement walls going up. The renovations were completed in 1970.

Sometime after it was completed, W.F. Benge photographed the Sue Bennett Memorial School. The man standing in front of what Sue Bennett College now calls the Lewis Administration Building is not identified. The building was completed in 1897, and classes began in the building that year. This photograph is included courtesy of the University of Louisville Photographic Archives.

This is a 1960 aerial photograph of the Sue Bennett College campus. Methodist women's groups from various states built cottages (named after the states), some of which were still on campus when this photograph was taken. Four of the cottages can be seen in the lower right corner, which is the current location of the library and Student Center. In the school's early days, when it was an elementary and high school, entire families would move onto campus while their children were in class and live in the cottages. Sue Bennett College was established in 1896, and the first building was completed in 1897. Classes were held in the Laurel Seminary building on North Main Street until the building—recently named for the school's first president (then called superintendent), J.C. Lewis—was finished.

The Laurel Seminary building was completed in 1858, the contract having been signed in 1856. The General Assembly had, in the latter part of the eighteenth century, granted counties land in the western part of the state that they could sell and use the proceeds for the establishment of local schools. Classes were held in the building through the end of the nineteenth century, with the Sue Bennett Memorial School holding its first semester of classes in the building in 1896. It was used as a military hospital during the War between the States. The building was expanded for use by the London Grade School in the early part of the twentieth century. The grade school was demolished in 1957 to make room for the construction of the current grade school on the site. The top photograph, made by W.F. Benge, is included courtesy of the University of Louisville Photographic Archives. The creator of the photograph below is unknown.

The kindergarten class of 1954–55 at the London Grade School consisted of the following students, from left to right: (front row) unknown, Paige Dyche, Helen Hackney, Beth Wilson, Pam Watkins, Judy Sharp, Vicky Nelson, and Mary Ann Fiechter; (middle row) Linda Fiechter, Carl Keith Greene, Dicky Doane, Berry Cupp, Ernie Cornett, Juddy Oakes, Durwood House, and Clyde Barton; (back row) Jimmy Sutton, Harold Henson Miller, Tim McFadden, Jimmy Hibbard, unknown, Ted Williams, Bobby King, and teacher Lorene Barton.

The students of this 1955–56 first grade class at the London Grade School are, from left to right, as follows: (front row) Larry Harber, Berry Riley, Brady Brummett, Barbara Mills, Durwood House, Tommy Larkey, and Linda Riley; (middle row) Freida Kelly, Wanda Cheek, Valeria Gregory, unknown, Jimmy Hibbard, and James Witt; (back row) Larry Hampton, Carl Wayne Hale, Faye Marcum, Eddie Collier, Johnny Cooper, Linda Ooten, Bill Manning, and teacher Laura Chesnut. The school was integrated in this school year.

The light-colored front portion of this building was built as an addition to the front of the Laurel Seminary building in 1908. In 1921 the darker addition was built around the old seminary building; the shell of the older building served as the new addition's central hallway, and the staircases of the older structure connected the new addition to the 1908 building. Classes for both the grade school and the high school were held here until the new high school (below) was built in 1936. The building was razed and a new grade school building was built in 1957.

The new London High School was built by the Works Progress Administration in 1936 and served as the city high school until the city and county schools merged in 1970.

Molly Young Smith was one of the
outstanding educators in London in the
middle part of the twentieth century. She
taught Latin and English. This photograph
was made in about 1923, probably by her
father, P.L. Young, who was a local
commercial photographer.

Professor H.V. McClure, affectionately
called "Prof. McClure," served as the
superintendent of London schools from
1935 to 1945. He was president of the
Upper Cumberland Educational
Association and the Kiwanis Club of
London, a member of Alpha Nu and Phi
Delta Kappa, and studied at the
University of Kentucky and the
University of New York.

A.J. "Jack" McCarty served as the band director at London High School from 1964 until 1969. Later he became director of the Laurel County High School's band. McCarty directed award-winning bands not only in Laurel County, but also in Glasgow and Clay Counties. While living in London he was also director of the adult choir at the First Christian Church.

John Patrick was McCarty's predecessor at London High as well as at the First Christian Church. Patrick was the band director at London High from 1962 to 1964.

Prior to 1955, schools in London, like most other schools in the nation, were segregated. London had what was called a Colored School District until 1955. These young men were photographed in the yard of the Colored School on North Mill Street by Tama Riley. They are, from left to right, Leonard Smith, Bobby McClain, Elroy Brown, Homer Smith, Cleon Elliot, John Cooper, and Gene Brown. The man behind Cooper could not be identified. The photograph below, of the entire student body and teachers, was taken sometime in the mid-1940s. Both photographs are from the collection of Tama Riley.

In the good old days there were four distinct high schools in Laurel County: London, Lily, Bush, and Hazel Green. There had been others: East Bernstadt, Long Branch, and Felts. This photograph shows the Lily High School class of 1934. Shown are, from left to right, as follows: (front row) Cleo Osborne, Robert Terrell, Mary Brock Sherman, Mary Jones Madden, Dora Taylor Tuttle, Delia Moore Nolan, Mae Wells, Hazel Black Britton, and Vivian Roberts Smith; (middle row) Raymond Hyden, Mayme Benge Carrico, Tommy Hyde, Lucy Woods Gibbons, Emma McVay Creech, Chrisa Benge Britton, Lucy Parsons Hopkins, Matt Brock, and Eddie Wilkerson; (back row) Ben Barker, Clyde Meadows, Eugene Killion, Archie West, and Jack Parsons.

Lily High School was consolidated with the rest of the county high schools in 1970, and the grade school there was closed in 1994, when it and the Felts Grade School were merged to form the new Hunter Hills Elementary School.

The Rhythm Band of the 1954–55 London kindergarten class was photographed just before a concert. The students are identified on p. 62. The kindergarten, which met in the London Grade School building, was sponsored by the London Women's Club.

The 1958–59 kindergarten class posed for its graduation photo on May 26, 1959, at London's First Baptist Church. Shown are, from left to right, as follows: (front row) Michael Kent Smith, Gerald Moores, Jeffrey Payne, Kenny Rayfield, Doris Douglas, Ava Jaunzems, Denny Jones, Terry Timberlake, Allison Oates, Joyce Ball, and Monica Adams; (back row) Steve Chesnut, Peggy Ann Fiechter, Karen Sue Cantrill, Harold Benge, Mark Adams, Barbara Seeley, Mary Dupree, Debbie Congleton, Debbie Benge, Libby Isaacs, Kay Humfleet, and Louise Isaacs.

In May 1961 London's Girl Scout Troop 2, which met at the First Baptist Church, studied Red Cross First Aid and commemorated the event with a photograph. The girls are, from left to right, as follows: (front row) Cherri Turner, Rose Sharon Patton, Judy Brown, Jeanette Jones, Shirley House, Red Cross instructor Pauline Patton, and Rebecca Samples; (kneeling, on either side of the American flag) Christy Hamm and Norma Sutton; (standing) Laura Susan Tyree, troop leader Ruth Milby, Linda Wayne Reep, Sallie Pennington, and Sue Ann Thompson.

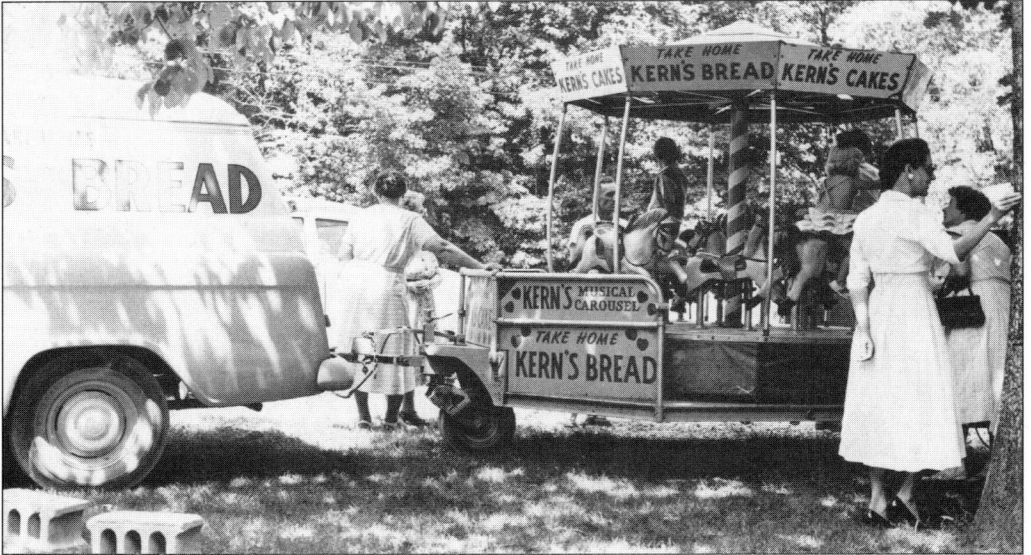

In the 1950s and 1960s Kern's Bakery used this children's carousel as a promotional tool, taking it to schools, picnics, festivals, and other such events. It was a big hit with the kids. Oscar "Junior" Ellison was usually its operator.

The 1955–56 London Women's Club kindergarten posed on the steps of the London Grade School for this April 1956 photograph. Shown are, from left to right, as follows: (front row) unknown, Ray Heuser, Susan Chesnut, Jack Luker, Pat Hogan, Gail Griffin, and Danny Hagedorn; (middle row) Becky Bowling, Karen Jones, Janice Ellison, Betty Prewitt, David Ison, Margaret House, and Terry Cromer; (back row) Pat Jones, Nicky Hensley, Susie Moberly, Bill Combs, Nannette Curry, Charlotte Rawlings, and Lorene Barton.

In the winter of 1959–60 London saw some of the heaviest snowfalls in more than a decade. These photographs of "Oaklawn," then owned by the Russell Dyche family, were made during that snowfall, which stayed on the ground for well over a month. The home had been occupied earlier by W.B. Catching who, at the turn of the century, was one of the leading forces in the old Star Route mail contracting business. Catching built the Catching Building between East Fifth and East Fourth Streets. Dyche was the owner and editor of *The Sentinel-Echo* and one of its predecessors, the *London Sentinel*. The home was razed in about 1970 to make way for the Carnaby Square shopping center on South Main Street.

McCalla FitzGerald, a cashier at the old First National Bank, lived in the home above at the turn of the century, when it appeared in the *Views of London* pamphlet. It stood on the corner of North Main and West Tenth Streets and eventually became the home of Judge W.E. Begley. It was razed in the early 1960s to make way for the gasoline station that is currently owned by Roy Schott. The home below was owned by J.C. McKee when it appeared in *Views of London*. It stood on the corner of South Long and West Third Streets and was replaced by an apartment building in the 1960s. The flat space on the roof that appears to be a widow's walk was actually a platform where McKee, an amateur astronomer, set up his telescopes.

The London Manufacturing Company was photographed sometime around the turn of the century by W.F. Benge. No record can be found of the location of the business, though it is probable that it was located near the railroad, perhaps on North Main Street. There seems to be a church steeple in the distance behind the utility pole in the middle of the photograph, which may put the business on the southwest side of town. The company's raw material appears to be lumber. This photograph is included courtesy of the University of Louisville Photographic Archives.

The Laurel Feed Mill building stood on this site on East Fourth (Manchester) Street from the time this photograph was made, sometime around the turn of the century, until 1995, when it was razed. The photograph shows that the store sold flour, meal, feed, grain, and hay. The lower area has a sign advertising a fine livery and feed stable. The store's phone number was 143.

Ray Humfleet operated a body shop, a wrecker service, and an auto parts business on US 25, south of town, into the 1960s. Humfleet eventually became a realtor and auctioneer, and operated his realty company in the building. It now houses the Ford Realty and Auction Company, which Humfleet merged with in the 1990s. This photograph was made in the 1960s. The automobile on the roof is a real Model-T Ford. It once had a mannequin inside waving to passers-by.

These views of the intersection of US 25 and KY 229, south of London, were made on the same day. In the center of the image above is the building that housed the Hatcher Motor Co. when the picture was taken, and that now houses the Philpot Tire Co. The next building to the right is Hall's Supermarket. The Gulf station that is shown on the extreme right of the photograph above and on the left in the photograph below was operated by Walton Rudder. The garage to its right is Sam's Garage, owned by Sam Parker. The Southmoor Motel advertised on the billboard was located on North Main Street. Main Street was US 25, the nation's first main north-south highway on the west side of the Appalachian Mountains. From London, motorists had the choice of traveling due south on US 25 and US 25W toward Knoxville, or veering east on KY 229 to US 25E through the Cumberland Gap if they were headed to the east coast.

One of London's earliest manufacturing companies in the modern era was London Church Furniture. This photograph shows the company's building on US 25, south of London, in the early 1970s. Earl Abbott and associates started the business in the 1950s. Now his son David runs the business and makes church furniture for churches across the country. The building burned in the late 1980s and the company moved to a new location on KY 80, west of town.

The Avalon Cheese Company began making cheese from local milk in 1964, and operated for more than a decade before going out of business. The plant was located in East London.

The Dixie Tobacco Warehouse was built in the 1950s. Tobacco was sold through the warehouse into the 1970s. The building was torn down in the 1980s and has been replaced with retail businesses and a bank branch.

The Kentucky State Police post in London was completed in 1949 at the intersection of KY 80 and US 25. It was replaced with a modern structure in 1977.

Forest fire lookout towers like this one once stood watch over national and state forests across the nation. This one, at Baldrock, was removed in the 1970s, when the forest outgrew it and aircraft came into common use in fire detection. The tower, just off KY 192, west of London, had a popular picnic area at its base.

Cumberland Dairies opened its Snack Bar in the early 1950s, and it remained a local eatery into the late 1960s. The Snack Bar was located on North Main Street opposite Cook Bros. Auto Parts, which can be seen, together with its sign advertising that it was "air cooled," reflected in the window. The Snack Bar became a popular lunch site for London High students.

Finley's Drive-in restaurant opened south of town on US 25, near the Levi Jackson Park entrance, in the 1950s, and served as a gathering place for teenagers. This photograph was made in the 1970s, just before the drive-in closed. The restaurant is on the extreme right-hand side of the photograph. It boasted space for autos under the scalloped canopy, and also space for another hundred cars behind the building. The water tank in the background provided water for the Caron Spinning Company.

The Dairy Dart was another place teenagers gathered at in the 1950s and 1960s. This photograph was made in the 1960s, obviously around Christmas. The restaurant, on South Main Street, is still in business and boasts the best foot-long hot dog in town.

In 1968 these men cut the ribbon to celebrate the opening of London's newly renovated airport, Magee Field. Shown on the left, watching, is FAA Flight Service Station Chief Bob Cushman. At the ribbon are Leon Ballard, Governor Louie Nunn, Paul Jones, Bea Campbell, and Gene Smith. W.S. Carpenter is looking on.

This aerial photograph of the airport was made before the field's main services were moved to the south side of the field.

WFTG Radio news reporter Jim Parman interviews Governor Louie Nunn, who cut the ribbon. Parman was the radio station's morning man from the 1960s into the early 1970s.

The airport's 6,000-foot runway can handle almost any type of aircraft. This photograph shows a Federal Aviation Administration aircraft parked on the apron, with a Piedmont Airlines YS-11 preparing to taxi onto the active runway. The airport was opened in 1956 and continued regular airline service into the 1980s. Today it is one of the busiest general aviation airports in the state.

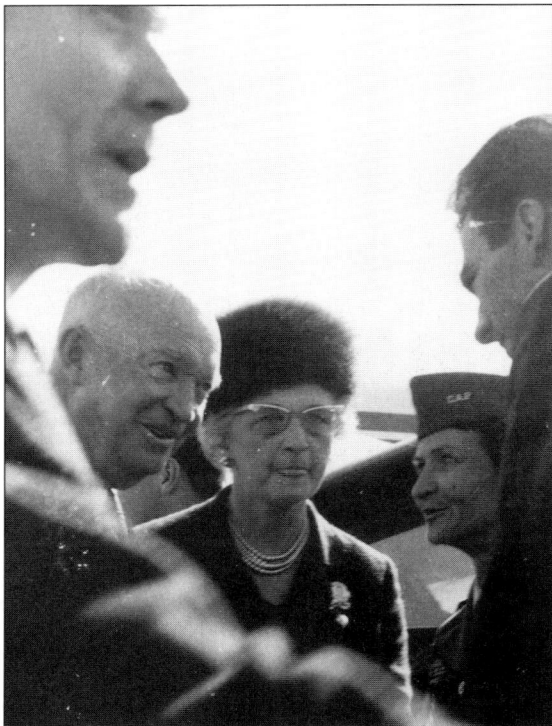

In 1962 former President Dwight D. Eisenhower visited London's airport to stump for the reelection of Thruston B. Morton to the U.S. Senate. This photograph shows Eisenhower and London's Opal Lucas, then a member of the Republican National Committee, greeting visitors at that event behind the protective arm of a security person. Also visible to the right of Lucas is Civil Air Patrol Captain Pauline Patton.

The London Squadron Civil Air Patrol was organized during World War II. The squadron met in the terminal building of the airport prior to building its own headquarters in the late 1960s. This photograph, made about 1967, shows the squadron's cadet corps. Shown are, from left to right, as follows: (kneeling) Carl K. Greene, Danny Abbott and Roger Garrison; (standing) Harold H. Miller, Bobby Gray, Donnie Lincks, Linda House, Jim Depew, Elaine House, Joe Isgrigg, and William Paul Wells.

Six

Looking at the People of London

In 1961 Police Chief John Noe (center), Mayor George Sutton (right), and police officer Oscar Westerfield displayed the city's new police car. Noe served as police chief for at least two decades. Sutton was mayor for two terms. Behind Sutton is the Chappell's Dairy distribution center.

At a meeting of the minds in the late 1960s at the London Country Club, London banker Warren "Butch" Little (with his back to the camera) talked with Fifth District Congressman Tim Lee Carter (left), and Carter's local representative Robert I. "Bob" Morgan of London. Carter retired in the early 1970s. Little was CEO of the Cumberland Valley National Bank.

In 1973 Sheriff Les Yaden was sworn in by Laurel Circuit Judge Robert Helton. Yaden was a retired Kentucky State Police detective and was the first democrat to be elected Laurel County sheriff since 1921, when Emmitt Stringer was elected. Helton served from 1969 to 1983. The photograph was made in the Laurel Circuit Courtroom.

Charles Gabbard, shown here with his wife Ollie, served as circuit court clerk from 1951 to 1969. He had served in the same post in Jackson County prior to moving to Laurel and served as a deputy clerk before running for office here.

Laurel County Judge John D. Gross Jr. served from 1965 to 1973. While he was judge a new Laurel County Jail was built and Laurel County saw great industrial development. Prior to entering into public service Gross operated a lumber business. His father had previously served in the same office for sixteen years.

O.J. Minnix, a businessman, was Laurel County circuit clerk from 1939 to 1945. He and H.V. McClure owned the Southland Theatre together for a while. Minnix was the sole owner when it burned in the spring of 1950. He also owned a bakery on West Seventh Street behind the Hotel Laurel, and for a while owned the bus station in London. During the Eisenhower administration he was appointed to a position in the United States Post Office Department and lived in Washington, D.C. until his death.

Fred V. Lucas was a state representative from Laurel County from 1929 until 1931. He was the youngest man in the House of Representatives during his term. Lucas dealt in real estate and was a local businessman, at one time owning the local Buick dealership. He also served as Laurel County sheriff from 1937 to 1941, and in the state senate from 1955 to 1959.

George Bruner was Laurel County clerk from 1937 to 1953. He was also on the board of the First National Bank and owned an insurance agency. Bruner was a 33rd degree Mason and in 1954 was chairman of the Laurel County Library Board. He started his career as a school teacher and in 1932 began working as a deputy county clerk. In 1937 he was elected to the office.

Henry Walden was George Bruner's deputy clerk and was elected to the office in 1953. He held this office until 1982. Walden, also a businessman, owned the local Chevrolet dealership. He is a Clay County native and moved here with his parents when he was six years old.

Roy Tooms was one of the quiet men in London who did good things without talking much about it. He was a lawyer and had served six years as an FBI agent before opening his practice in London. After leaving the FBI in 1947, he practiced law and was the city judge in Barbourville for a couple of years before coming to London. Tooms served on the London City School Board, was active as an adult leader in the Boy Scouts, and in 1954 was cubmaster for the London Cub Scout Pack. He was also active in the Methodist church and the London Lions Club.

Conrad F. Handy was one of London's most active promoters and supporters. He was in the motel business for several years and promoted London as a tourist destination as well as a nice place to stay on your way to somewhere else. He was a member of the Kiwanis Club of London. His sons, Jim and Tom, are also active in the tourism industry in London.

Dr. Boyce E. Jones came to London in 1949 and opened his practice here. He specialized in respiratory diseases and was not only on the staff of Marymount Hospital, but also on the staff of the state tuberculosis hospital in London. When he retired to Florida, he pursued his favorite hobby, fishing. Jones was active in the recruitment of new physicians to London when there was a shortage in the mid-1960s. He and physicians such as Sam Adams, D.D. Turner, C.A. Wathen, and Bob Pennington worked many hours of overtime, taking care of London's citizens when there were few physicians who wanted to set up a practice here.

Dr. James E. McCracken Sr. opened his optometric practice in London in 1952 on the second floor of the Poynter Building, where this photograph was made. In the 1960s he built his own building on the corner of West Fifth and Broad Streets where he practiced until his death in 1970. His son, James Jr., took over the practice. Dr. McCracken Sr. was active in local civic affairs, a member of the London Lions Club, and a Jaycee.

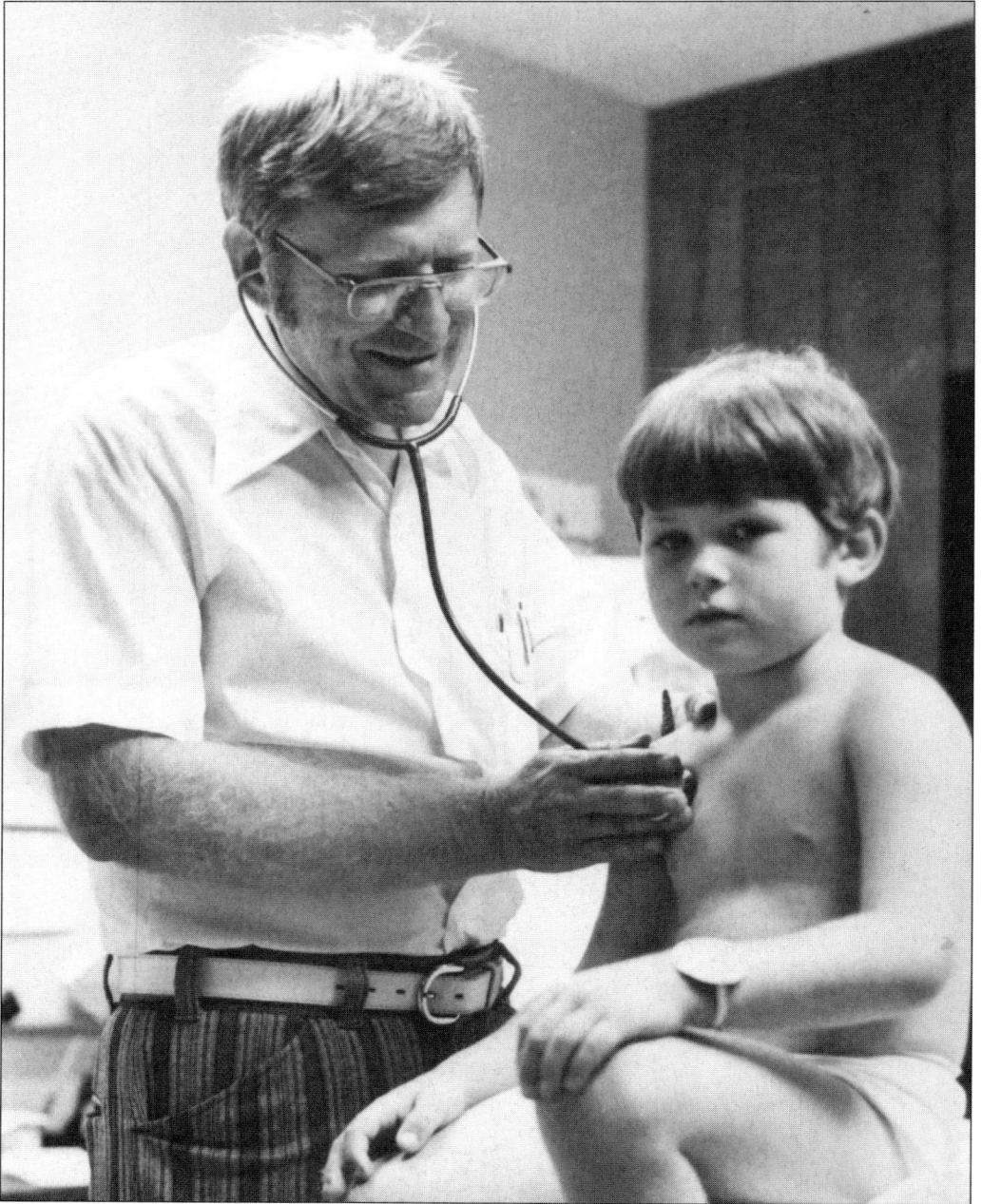

Dr. Paul R. Smith, London's senior physician, came to London in 1960. He has served as chief of staff at Marymount Hospital and president of the Kentucky Academy of Family Practice. Dr. Smith has been active in the expansion of medical facilities in London and has served on the board of Marymount Hospital. He, as well as Dr. Jones and their contemporaries, was active in the recruitment of new physicians to London when there was a shortage. He is a member of the London Lions Club and has served on the official board of London's First Christian Church. The boy he is shown examining in this early 1970s photograph could not be identified, despite the author's efforts.

In the winter of 1929 J.W. Terry, George Terry, an unidentified man, and Finley Hurley hitched a horse to the London Laundry truck to get it unstuck from a snow bank. J.W. Terry started London Laundry in August 1927, and it stayed in his family until August 1987, when his nephew, Jack Timberlake, sold it to Coyne Textiles.

That same winter Finley Hurley used a wagon to deliver linen to Begley Drug. He is shown here with the Poynter Building and London Hardware in the background. The sign on the building next to London Hardware proclaims the business to be the "Tourist Cafe," which boasted cooked meals.

Cecil Yeary (left) and Don Edwards (right) flank Caron Spinning Company officials as they prepare to break ground for the Caron plant on US 25, south of London. The location of Caron here in the early 1960s kicked off an industrial expansion boom in London that saw companies such as Phoenix Manufacturing, Micro Devices, and Rotary Manifold open new plants.

Ford salesmen R.C. Walker (left) and Ernest "Fats" Tincher (right) were presented the Ford Top Hatter Award by the London Motor Car Co. (owner Roy McWhorter is at center) just after the 1964 Ford Falcon hit the showroom floor.

These air traffic control specialists at the FAA's Flight Service Station at London's airport were apparently being honored for their service at the facility when this photograph was made in the 1960s. Shown are, from left to right, Ken Macht, Bob Johnson, Al Wilson, Carl Neeley, Mack Jones, and Rola Vice.

On July 1, 1959, London lawyer William Hamm (seated at center), president of the J.M. Feltner 4-H Club Camp, was presented with a check for $20,000 by John L. Bruner, treasurer of the Laurel County 4-H Club Council, for construction of the camp. The check represented a donation from Laurel County businesses. Russell Dyche (seated at left) promised to match the businesses' contributions if they raised at least $10,000. Seated at right is Woodrow McIntosh, then of Pineville and Hamm's predecessor as president. Standing next to Bruner is George Corder of Lexington, a UK Extension Service 4-H agent.

In 1969 the London High cheerleaders posed for photographs advertising Chappell's Milk for ads in the football and basketball programs and the high school paper, the *Londonian*. Shown from left to right are as follows: (kneeling) Jennifer George, Gail Yaden, and Sharon Faulkner; (standing) Monica Adams, Mary Dupree, and Jan Gilbert.

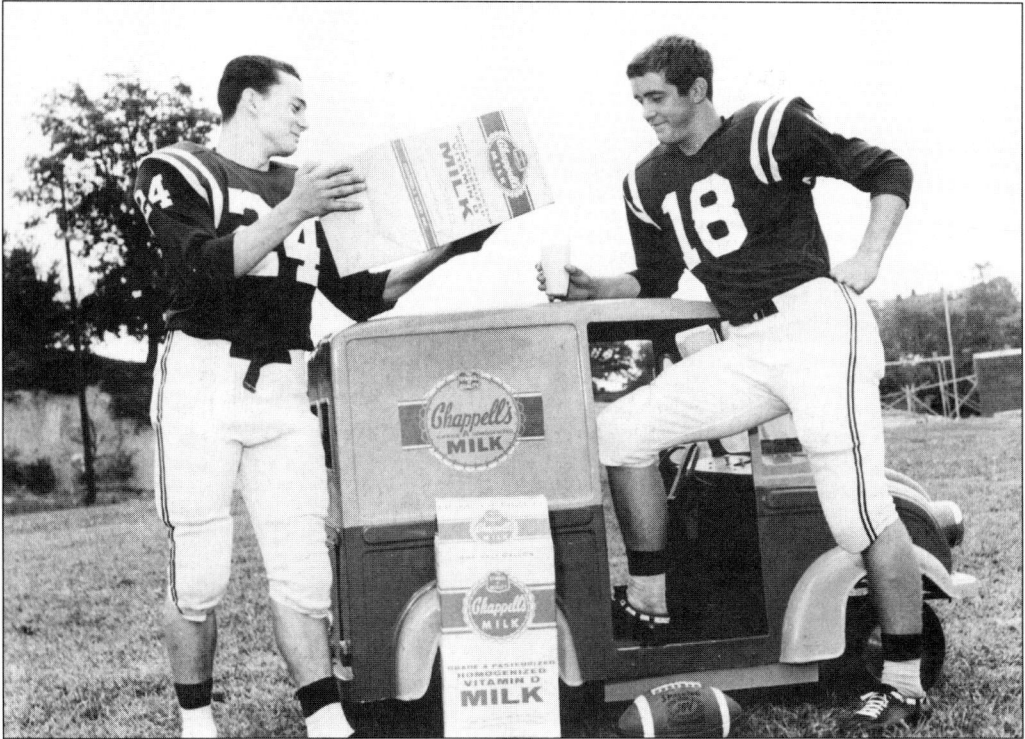

Five years earlier, in 1963, Phil Lowrey and Don Houchens refreshed themselves with Chappell's Milk at a miniature milk delivery truck used in an advertisement. Chappell's merged with a dairy marketing cooperative to form the Flav-o-rich company.

Four coaches and a principal met sometime before 1964 to draw for pairings in the 48th District High School Basketball Tournament. Shown from left to right are Lily High Coach Harold Storm, London High Principal Leighton Watkins (holding the hat), Hazel Green High Coach Sam Karr, London High Coach Gilbert "Mutt" Samples, and Bush High Coach Joe Tom Gregory.

This is the 1935–36 London High basketball team. Shown from left to right are as follows: (seated) Nolan Kidd, Jimmy Williams, Bill Triplett, Gilmore Phelps, Vernon House, and Ralph Hammons; (standing) Biscuit Eversole, manager, Dan McFadden, Warren Baker, Willard Phelps, Eathel "Pete" House, Charles Gaines, and coach Clyde "Buzz" Greene.

Twenty-nine years later, London High honored these athletes at its annual athletic banquet. Shown from left to right are Bill Dalton, Bobby Davis, Sherrie Adams, Ronnie Minnix, David Brown, David Van Leuven, Wayne Bennett, Tom Harkleroad, Bobby Waldroff, and Phillip Lowry.

The 1934–35 Lily High basketball team included, from left to right: (front row) coach Jarvis Parsley, Floyd Powers, Alton Burnett, Virgil Black, and manager Carl Bryant; (back row) Casper Hopkins, Walton Burnett, Thurman Burnett, Willie Root, and Earl Killion.

In 1961 Lily High won the 12th Region High School Basketball Tournament. Here Monticello High coach Joe Harper, a London native, presents the championship trophy to Harvey Mize as Johnny Owens looks on. Lily lost to Louisville's Seneca High School in the first round of the state tournament. It was Lily's only trip to the Sweet Sixteen. Bush preceded Lily and played in the 1950 tournament, losing to Campbellsville in the first round. London High made it to state tournaments in 1924, 1925, 1947, 1944, and 1948. In 1927 the Tigers lost to the Millersburg Military Institute in the finals. Hazel Green played in state tournaments in 1933, 1934, 1940, 1942, 1947, 1965, 1966 and 1970, and won the state championship in 1940.

In a photograph made in May 1961, these eight golfers pose next to the temporary clubhouse at the London Country Club. Shown from left to right are Warren "Butch" Little, Wally Rose, Howard Jones, unknown, Bill Lear, Johnny Owens (who won several state amateur championships), Roy Moore, and Judson Oakes. The country club was established in 1959 and the current clubhouse was built in the late 1960s.

The London Firemen's Band posed perhaps in 1938, prior to hosting The Cumberland Valley Band Festival on the Sue Bennett Memorial School campus. The festival included twelve bands and was broadcast on WHAS radio in Louisville. The band's director was John Griffey (at right). The band was organized in 1932 and existed until 1938, when the London High School band was organized. Many of the young people in this photograph were probably in the first London High band.

London's Parman family posed for this photograph in the early 1960s. Shown from left to right are the Parman brothers (Goebel, Larkin, John, Robert, Ed, and Albert); their sisters Alma and Hettie (seated on either side of their stepmother, who they called Aunt Mandy); and Bob Parman's grandson, Bobby Joe (kneeling).

Sallie Black, Florence Underwood, and Thelma Black look back at the camera in this c. 1923 photograph taken on the top of town hill on Whitley Road (now called Keavy Road), KY 363. The city of London can be seen in the background.

This photograph of the W.J. Chesnut family was made in 1963 on the Chesnuts' 50th wedding anniversary. From left to right are as follows: (seated) Ruby (Mrs. Jennings) Chesnut, Christine Chesnut Clotfelter, Mr. and Mrs. W.J. Chesnut, Pauline Chesnut (Mrs. Dyche) Jones, Madge (Mrs. Don) Chesnut, and Sarah Chesnut; (standing) Jennings Chesnut, Jack Clotfelter, Paula Jo Clotfelter, Stephen Chesnut, Don Chesnut, Don Chesnut Jr., Carol Thomas Chesnut, William Chesnut, Susan Chesnut, Bruce Chesnut, Shirley Chesnut, Dyche Jones, and Donna and Bill Frank Jones.

Ray Lewis and his mother Alice are shown here in the 1960s. Mr. Lewis, a lawyer, served two terms as Laurel Circuit Judge. He was elected in 1945 and 1951. This photograph was shot on the stairs leading to the second floor of the Poynter Building.

The Begley family, founders of the Begley Drug Store chain, posed in 1969, at the birthday of their mother, Mrs. W.E. Begley (seated at left). Shown standing are Opal Begley, Ernest Ray Begley, Bob Bruce Begley, Vera Begley and Shirley Begley. Seated in front of Vera Begley is Uncle Henry Dyche, and to the right is Martin Dyche.

105

Alfred Fiechter (second from the left in the front row) came to Laurel County from Bern, Switzerland, with his parents in 1881, when he was twelve years old. He married Rosa Trosch (seated next to him) and they had ten children. Flanking their parents are Frederick and Walter; standing are Herman, William, Martha, Paul Frederich, Bertha, Ernest, Flora, and Albert.

Several decades later, in December 1961, Alfred's son, Paul Frederich, posed with his family. He and his wife, Annie Mae Gumm Fiechter, are in the middle of the couch. On either side of them are Rosa Virginia and Thelma Marie. Standing behind them are Roberta Louise, Ina Mae, Ercel Alfreda, Julia Irene, Paul Woodrow, Donald George, William Alfred, and Conrad Abner.

106

Seven
Remembering London's Tourist Stopovers

London's location, about half a day's drive from Cincinnati and a day's drive from Michigan and the shore of Lake Erie, makes it a perfect place to stop over on the way south, so London boasts a plethora of motels. That was true in the past as well. The Village Motel on North Main Street, featuring country ham and hot biscuits in its restaurant, was torn down in the early 1970s to make way for the shopping center that then housed Kmart and Kroger's. Though several motels have been razed, more than enough have been built to replace them.

London Hall's restaurant also featured country ham and hot biscuits. The hams, though, were cured in the restaurant itself. The next four photographs show London Hall from the mid-1940s into the early 1960s. The photograph above shows the restaurant in 1944 or 1945, near the end of the World War II. By the time the photograph below was made in the late 1940s the awning had been taken down from above the gas pumps and the gasoline brand had changed from Sinclair to Conoco.

By the time the top photograph was made in the 1950s, London Hall's gas pumps were gone and so were the overhanging porches. The south end provided space to hang hams for curing, a new entrance had been built, and a new circular addition had been made on the north end of the restaurant. New signage had been put up, and the restaurant had been installed with air-conditioning. The photograph below shows the restaurant in the early 1960s. London Hall was known around the area as a place for fine food and southern fried chicken. In the 1950s a motel was built across the street from the restaurant.

London Hall's country hams were so famous that in the early 1960s the restaurant's owner, Bobby Curry (right), presented one of them to then Governor Bert T. Combs. Combs was a Clay County native and one of a few governors elected from eastern Kentucky. In the photograph below bathers enjoy the new pool built at London Hall in the early 1950s. The London Hall pool was London's first public pool.

The 4-Paw Hotel on North Main Street next to the First Christian Church was still in business in the 1970s, but was eventually razed after the church bought the property. The hotel structure incorporated the home built by Al Aikman sometime before 1870. The gable on the left is apparently part of that home. Joe Stillwell purchased the home from Colonel R.L. Ewell and made it into a hotel. In about 1930 it was bought by Mr. and Mrs. Shropshire, who changed the name to 4-Paw, for the circus Mr. Shropshire had operated.

The Dog Patch Bargain Barn was opened by the House family in about 1947, 7 miles north of London on US 25, and named for the fictional town in the Al Capp comic strip, Li'l Abner. The souvenir shop became a popular stop for tourists on the main north-south route through Kentucky. It has even outlived the comic strip for which it was named. The shop has subsequently moved to a location at the I-75 interchange north of London and is currently operated by Bobby and Cleta Jones.

From the beginning of the construction of I-75, until the final stretch was completed from London to Corbin, traffic volume on US 25, London's Main Street, increased drastically. As a result, business boomed at service stations such as this one, House and Brown Texaco, operated by Charles "Bill" House and Luther "Crow" Brown. In the mid and late 1960s traffic on summer holiday weekends was so heavy, and travel through London so slow, that passengers could get out of their vehicle while it was still in traffic and go into a grocery store such as Grimes' Grocery (at the right of the photograph). They were able to buy drinks and snacks and to catch up with their car before it got very far up the road. This photograph appears to have been made about 1960. The station was near the corner of North Main and Sixteenth Streets.

Eight

Levi Jackson Wilderness Road State Park

Levi Jackson Wilderness Road State Park has been the site of millions of picnics, horse shoe matches, family reunions, and sixty Laurel County Homecomings. The park was opened in 1935, and this clubhouse was built on the hill overlooking the amphitheatre at the top of the hill that leads into the park. When this clubhouse fell victim to a fire about 1950, a new clubhouse was built on the opposite hill overlooking the amphitheatre to be used as a dining facility for the group camp built there. The newer clubhouse also burned in 1995 and was rebuilt on the same site in 1996.

McHargue's Mill has been the centerpiece of the park since its construction soon after the park's opening in 1935. The mill, with an "undershot" turbine wheel, contains mill parts that were in operation on Robinson Creek in 1812, and was featured in the motion picture *The Kentuckian*. It was recently refurbished and during the summer corn is ground as a demonstration project for park visitors. The mill can process both corn and wheat.

This view of the mill shows the pond impounded by the mill's dam on the Little Laurel River. In *The Kentuckian*, the character played by Burt Lancaster ran "across" the pond. Actually, he was supported by a wire net suspended a few inches below the level of the pond. Recently, the park's collection of millstones was catalogued and displayed on the banks of the pond.

114

The parts of the old Johnson Mill were displayed for a few years under a shelter alongside the mill. This postcard view was made sometime in the 1940s.

The winter of 1959–60 was one of the snowiest London experienced during that era, and some enterprising photographer made this photograph of the snow-covered mill. The rail in the foreground is the railing for the bridge across the Little Laurel River on the park's entrance road.

The Mountain Life Museum at Levi Jackson Wilderness Road State Park developed along with the park. The photograph above is from about 1935 and was probably made about the time the park was opened. The museum was still under construction when the photograph below was made. The foundation for one of the buildings can be seen in the lower right. The museum celebrates the lifestyle of the pioneers who came to this area and settled here. The buildings are all original log structures moved to the park from other sites in the county.

In 1955 the Mountain Life Museum was converted to the town of "Prideville," for the motion picture *The Kentuckian*, based on the novel *The Gabriel Horn*, and starring Burt Lancaster. Local people were recruited as extras in the film. This photograph of a wardrobe test shows, from left to right, Londoners George Goss, Emery Evans, Sam Herrod, Tom Handy (in front of Herrod), Junior Lucas, and Jim Handy. The man at right was one of the professional actors in the film. Goss was taken to Hollywood to help promote the film and appeared on a segment of the Steve Allen Show.

The Levi Jackson Clubhouse has been the scene of many political gatherings. This photograph, probably made in 1959, shows former Governor A.B. "Happy" Chandler speaking at right. The rest of the photograph depicts members of the London High School band, apparently recruited to provide music for the event. Shown from left to right are Bobby Jones, Don Lane Young, Frankie Lane, Joyce Parrish, Jim Handy, Johnny Buchanan, Tom Handy, Jimmy Cottongim, and Jimmy Holmes. Three faces that are only partially visible could not be identified.

Nine
Remembering Laurel County Homecomings

In 1962 the Laurel County Homecoming Parade was only a few years old. Although the Homecoming celebration had been in existence since 1935, the parade was a new twist in the 1960s. This parade shot also offers a good view of the east side of North Main Street. The Hackney's float at the right side of the photograph reminds the parade watchers that Hackney's had been in the clothing business since 1879 and the store was "Where Your Grandfather Traded."

In this Laurel County Homecoming Parade Kentucky Utilities promoted all-electric homes. The photograph was taken from the second floor of the Poynter Building. Begley Drug can be seen in the background.

The London High School band plays as it passes "Doc" Fred Townsend's City Drug Store. City Drug was a popular stopover after school for London High students. Its cozy booths and lending library were popular features of the old fashioned drug store. Identifiable in the band are majorettes Martha Tumpak (right), and Betty Mills (second from left). Band members who can be identified include Harold Lane (on trombone at left in the front rank), Shirley House (behind him on clarinet), Freddy Yaden (next to her on tenor saxophone) and possibly Mike Binder (next to him on trumpet).

Thousands lined Main Street to view the 1962 Laurel County Homecoming Parade. The London Fire Department's first-aid vehicle is visible in the lower left, and a convertible bearing a candidate for queen is just behind the band.

A decade later, in the early 1970s, Connie Pitman, a candidate for queen, rode on the 1926 LaFrance firetruck driven by the Laurel County Fire Department.

Entertainment has always been the keystone of the Homecoming celebration. The event was spawned as a result of the community singing and band concert at the official opening of the Levi Jackson Wilderness Road State Park. The entertainment runs the gamut from country and western music to classical and folk. In the photograph above, made in the early 1970s, The Kountry Kings provide country music. Some years there is a reenactment of the historical event that the founders of the state park hoped to memorialize, the massacre of the McNitt Party as they encamped on the site of the park in October 1786. The photograph below is of one of those dramatic programs from the 1970s.

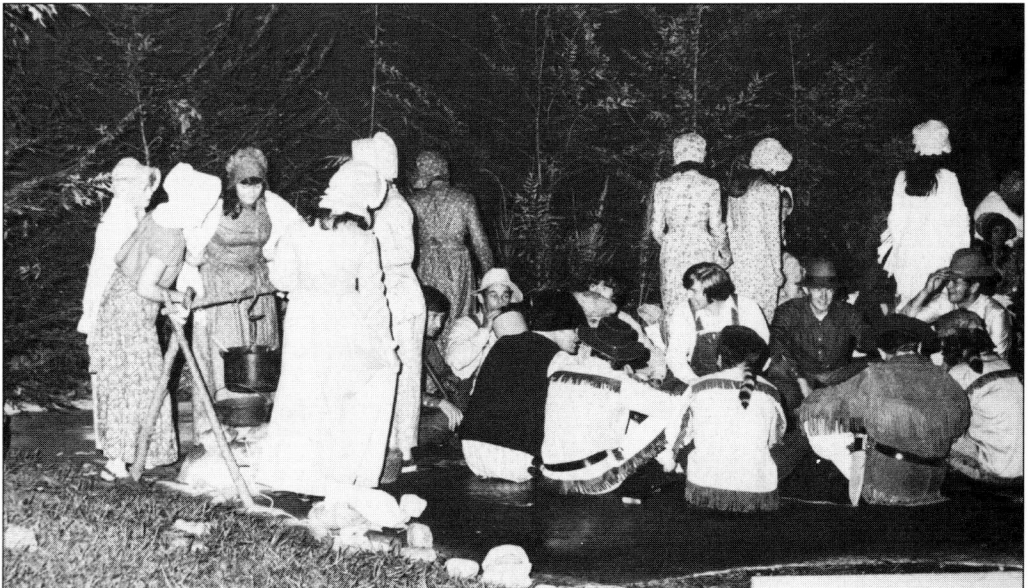

In the 1960s, one night of the three-day event, usually Friday night, was reserved for a variety show featuring local entertainers. The photograph at right shows London's Freddie Phelps and Ronnie Ingram in a tap dance. The young men were students of a local dance instructor. Other events traditionally include a beauty pageant, and on Sunday the Southeastern Kentucky Singing Convention.

In 1964 Gene Evans and Hazel Allen did a comedy act for the variety show. Mr. Evans was a realtor and auctioneer. The variety show was a chance to showcase local talent and give local entertainers a chance to get stage experience in the amphitheatre before audiences of up to ten thousand. The traditional date of the Homecoming is the weekend of the full moon in August, though in recent years this has been changed to the third full weekend in August. Traditionally, the event has covered Friday, Saturday, and Sunday, though for a while it ran for a full week. It currently runs Wednesday through Sunday.

Local civic clubs and church groups often find that operating a food or souvenir stand at the Homecoming can raise much money for their causes. This 1964 photograph shows the stand operated by the London Fireman's Club.

These members of the London Lions Club are shown here in 1964 preparing to sell snow cones at the Laurel County Homecoming. The Lions Club is one of London's older civic clubs.

This 1964 photograph shows members of the London Rotary Club preparing to sell their foods at the Laurel County Homecoming. The Rotary Club has been a community supporter for many years in London.

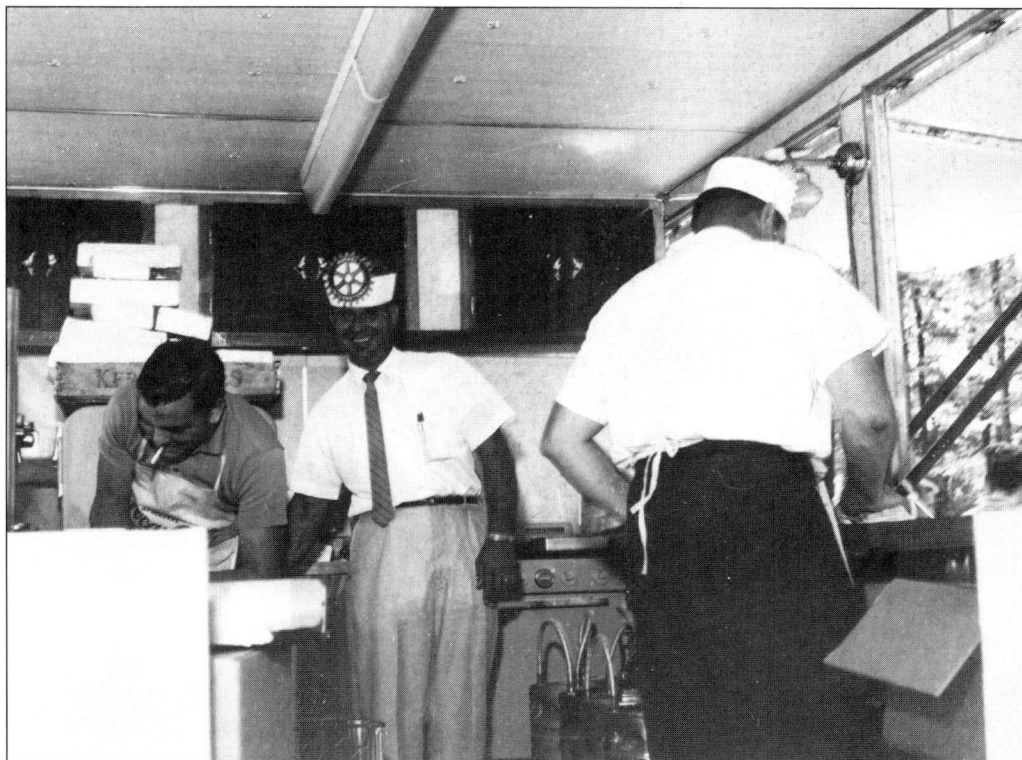

Since the mid-1950s a beauty pageant has been part of the Homecoming celebration. Some years the Homecoming beauty pageant was a Miss America preliminary. Most years it has been an independent pageant. In 1959 Barbara Hart (center) was named queen, and the runners-up were Shirley Green (left) and Frances Browning (right).

When rain was just too heavy to hold the pageants in the outdoor amphitheatre at the Levi Jackson Wilderness Road State Park, they were moved to the Belle Bennett Auditorium. In 1969 the rains came, and Nita Morris (second from left) was crowned queen. Runners-up were Debbie Conley (left), Mary Ann Chesnut, and Maggie Murray (right).

Acknowledgments

First I gratefully acknowledge the help and cooperation of my wife, Vaunene. She has put up with photographs being spread all over the kitchen, living room, and other parts of the house; my ignoring her while staring into the word processor; and my muttering to myself while I shuffled through photographs and notes. Her encouragement and understanding have been invaluable during the time I have worked on this book. Without her help this book would not have been possible. I thank her from the bottom of my heart.

I also appreciate all those who have contributed to my collection, and those who have remembered my collection when they have come across old photographs that they thought should be saved, but didn't want to keep themselves.

I extend my thanks to all those who have endured the phone calls I've made at odd hours asking unanswerable questions, and confirming dates and names. Thanks also go to those who have helped identify people and places in photographs. For that assistance thanks go to Sweetie Smith, Mr. and Mrs. John Paul Jones, Gilmore Phelps, Mr. and Mrs. Herschel Acton, Robert Dyche, Tom Handy, Marcia Ridings, Steve and Madge Chesnut, Bobby King, Dobbie Magee, Wilma Houchens, Gene Huff, Opal Mardis, Valerie Phelps, Raymond, Durwood and Darrell House, Gladys Minnix, Mary Ann Wilson, Barbara Lewis, Ed "Cutworm" Tincher, Judy Chaney, Roger Lewis, Lucille Elmore, Holbert Hodges, Lucille Holman, Barbara French, Mary Frances House, Mr. and Mr. Ray Brown, Fred Christian, Randell Rudder, Jackie McFadden, Jerry Weaver, Billie Ann Ridings, Dr. and Mrs. Paul Smith, and Jack Parman. Particular thanks goes to Thomas M. House.

I especially thank those who so kindly lent me some of the photographs I have used: Judge R.W. Dyche, Ellen Timberlake, Janice Ball, Terry Timberlake, Raymond Asher, and Tama Riley.